Q & A
from the heart
with John-Roger

Journal

Published by Mandeville Press
P.O. Box 3935, Los Angeles, California 90051

Printed in the United States of America
by BookCrafters, Chelsea, Michigan

I.S.B.N. 0-914829-28-9

Printed on recycled paper

Q: *If all things are happening according to the highest good and in perfect timing, why send the Light?*

A: *Because Spirit will not usually look at a plan to see if an alternate can be instituted unless requested from this level of Spirit. In the cosmic sense, taking all eternity into consideration, all things are ultimately for the highest good because not one Soul will be lost. But very few of us function at that cosmic, ultimate level. On this level where most of us function, all things don't seem to necessarily happen for the highest good or in perfect timing. So it's always appropriate to send the Light—for the highest good (which is something God knows and we, on our personality levels, don't always know). Sending the Light for the highest good increases the positive energy in a situation and increases the likelihood that, rather than a not-so-high good, the highest good possible will take place.*

Date:

Q: **I've heard you talk about the magnetic Light and the Light of the Holy Spirit. What is the difference?**

A: The magnetic Light relates to and can operate only in the levels below Soul. The Light of the Holy Spirit exists on the levels of Soul and above. It can and does come into the lower levels, riding the magnetic Light as a vehicle. Some of the ways you can know the difference between the two is that the Holy Spirit will never inflict itself on anything or anyone. It comes only where invited, and it operates for the highest good of all concerned. When you are doing anything different from that— trying to get someone to do something the way you want it done, trying to control the outcome of a situation, etc.— you are dealing with the magnetic Light, and there are always strings attached. When you stay out of areas of control and ask always for the highest good, you are more likely to be dealing with the Light of the Holy Spirit.

Date:

_____

_____

_____

_____

_____

_____

_____

_____

Date:

Q: *Many times when I think of you, I will send you the Light or say, "God bless you" to myself. Does this help you in any way?*

A: *Yes, it sure does. Thoughts are transmitted over long distances and we are affected on many different levels by them. Sending the thought "I love you" or "God bless you" can work wonders, and I appreciate it when you send those words to me.*

Date:

Date:

Q: **Would you share a little bit about Light columns?**

A: Let's just say that we should all be Light columns first. Physically, mentally, emotionally, spiritually, we should be a Light column. Then, wherever we go, wherever we sit, wherever we talk, we should leave a column of our beingness of Light there. We should project it collectively into areas so that we're just riveting everything together like a cobweb of Light forms, energies that are so intricately intertwined but as graceful as the most delicate lace. And even though they may look like a great whirlwind, sort of rough and crude, when you get into it, you find that it's a filigree and each little strand is very fine.

I don't know if you know it, but the steel that holds bridges up is made up of very small little strands that are woven together. It's not one big single piece of steel, because that would snap. The single strands give it flexibility of movement. And that flexibility is strength. The rigidity collapses. That's another way of saying that the law is rigid and grace is flexible.

Date:

Date:

Q: Is there any way to use the Light to protect the subconscious from being programmed when I'm not consciously aware that it is happening (television, advertising, etc.)?

A: The best way I know of to clean out subconscious or subliminal programming is spiritual exercises. During the early portion of s.e.'s, that which is in the subconscious is brought up to the surface for "airing." The more deeply rooted concepts are often handled in the middle part of s.e.'s; when you are reaching past the mind-chatter into the sound current, such programmed energies are often transmuted. The last third of s.e's are primarily for Soul transcendence and gaining awareness of the higher spiritual realms.

Date:

Date:

Q: *I have been reading a lot lately about the power of the subconscious mind and the power of thought. Exactly what is the power of thought and how important is thought in the "scheme of things"?*

A: *The best way to answer that is to tell you "energy follows thought." That means if you are thinking about a hot fudge sundae, all the levels of your consciousness come in line to bring that to you. The same is true for envisioning and moving toward higher awareness and Soul transcendence. All of your levels will start making that happen. You will receive cooperation from your mind, emotions, basic selves; even your subconscious will be guiding you though you will not be consciously aware of that level. That's why it becomes so important to watch your thoughts because you will create in a physical way those things you have focused on in your thinking. Also, be careful what you say. Listen to what you say and be sure it represents what you really want in your life.*

Date:

Date:

Q: *There are so many things that I don't understand about myself and the world. It all seems overwhelming. Where do I start?*

A: *Start with your next breath, and take one step at a time. When you look at yourself, if you see so many things you want to change that it's overwhelming, you might never start. So start with one thing. And when you have succeeded with that, you may decide to take on the next. Everything doesn't have to be changed overnight. Be patient with yourself, keep loving yourself and give yourself credit for the steps you are taking.*

The same can hold true when you look at "the state of the world." Start with yourself. Bring yourself into line first—one step at a time. Taking care of yourself or changing yourself could have profound effects on the rest of the world. But remember that you are not responsible for changing the entire world. Your main responsibility is to yourself.

Date:

Date:

Q: *How do I make a choice or find an answer that I know is for my highest good?*

A: *Sometimes when you ask God a question, and you ask "for your highest good," you won't get an answer—because that is for your highest good. Your spiritual teachers may want you to work through certain patterns a little bit longer so you will gain more experience, rather than opening the door and ushering you out of the situation. It's important to remember that what is positive from the spiritual point of view may not appear positive from the physical point of view. But when you honestly ask "for your highest good," your experiences will be for your highest good.*

Date:

Date:

Q: *I find that I often come across situations where I have trouble making decisions. Can you suggest a technique that might make this process easier?*

A: *One technique that may work is to "mock up" seeing through the eyes of a master. You can call in the Light, asking for perfect protection, and then go inside and ask what the master would do in this situation. You may find that the answers come, and they may be much more than just your own imagination. Then you can lean into what you have heard inwardly, and if it works for you, use it.*

Date:

Date:

Q: How can I know what is right or wrong for me?

A: Telling "right" from "wrong" can be a very fine line. One way to look at it would be that those things that accrue karma might be considered "bad" (although that may not always be true) and those things that keep you clear might be considered "good." But I'm not sure I know the difference between right and wrong. I know that what works for me, as long as it is noninflictive toward anyone else, could be considered "right." If an action is inflictive toward others, then I would say that you might call that "wrong."

Date:

Date:

Q: *What is evil?*

A: *My definition of evil is "unnecessary experience." The Soul is here to gain experience, but not all experience is necessary. Some things are a detour, a distraction and yet you must remember that not one Soul will be lost, so in the bigger picture, there is no unnecessary experience. It just depends on how many millions of existences you want to have experiences before you return to God.*

Date: _____

_____

_____

_____

_____

_____

_____

_____

_____

_____

_____

_____

_____

_____

Date:

Q: *No matter what I do I always have the feeling that I could have done better. What's going on?*

A: *The consciousness could be compared to an onion: layer upon layer upon layer. You peel off one layer of experience and you discover another layer. So you may sometimes find that the way you handled something, in what seemed to be the best you could do at a given time, in retrospect seems inadequate—because you have grown and discovered another layer within yourself that allows for a better solution. That feeling of "I could have done better" really points up your growth. You can view that as a positive step, not as a discouragement. Just keep moving. As long as you are still present on this earth, you will keep discovering more and more layers to work through—thank God. It's your process of unfoldment and evolvement into God.*

Date:

Date:

Q: *How can I know if I'm following my "purpose"? For instance, if God looked down at me, would He say, "Yeah, she's doing my will—she's doing what she should be doing." Or would He say, "She's just messing around. Won't she ever learn?"*

A: *If you are out of balance emotionally, mentally, financially or sexually, you are not doing what you've come here to do. This is something you can use as a guideline to let you know if you're "in line" with God's will or being "will-full." We are given the tools of the emotions and the mind to help guide us through our journey on this planet. When you experience an imbalance in any of these areas, that is an indicator that something is not quite right. A common response is to try to change your mind or "stuff" the emotions. But if you learn to listen and heed the signals being given, you can bring yourself back onto the path you have chosen and have greater abundance and freedom in your life.*

Date: _____

_____

_____

_____

_____

_____

_____

_____

Date:

Q: *I'm interested in meeting the Mystical Traveler inwardly and traveling out of my body. How can I best use the sound current I hear to move my consciousness away from my body?*

A: *What you are seeking to find actually takes place within you all the time. In reality, what you are learning to do is to become* more aware *of the times when you travel out of your body. This occurrence is not some action that is separate from you although many people have the mistaken concept that Soul awareness or the Traveler consciousness are something that takes place in an altered state of consciousness. It can take place while you are washing dishes, typing a letter or talking to a friend. It is a process of becoming more aware of who you truly are.*

Date:

Date:

Q: *What is Soul Transcendence?*

A: *The Soul is that essence of us that is a pure extension of God. The mind, emotions, and body are elements that the Soul has taken to itself in order to experience those levels of existence. In the course of our journey on earth, it is possible to learn not to be held in bondage—or restricted by—the body, mind, or emotions. And when those lower levels are transcended, that which is left is pure Soul. Eventually, as the journey back to God continues, Soul will also be transcended and there will be only God.*

Date:

Date:

Q: *What does it mean to be an initiate of the Mystical Traveler?*

A: *When you're initiated into the Sound Current, you are consciously working your way up through the different realms—the astral, causal (emotional), mental, etheric—and finally into Soul. You receive initiations into each level of consciousness, and the Traveler can then assist you in clearing a path through that level up into the next. It is sort of like boring a hole up through many layers of wood. When you have drilled a hole from one level into the next, you receive an initiation and start making a tunnel through that level, on into the Soul realm.*

To be an initiate of the Traveler is to devote yourself to the God within you, to devote yourself to Spirit, to returning to your home, the Soul Realm, from which you originally came before you incarnated onto this earth. It means devoting yourself to working out the karma you've accrued while being here and to releasing yourself from that karma through grace and your good works, so that you are free to rise into the heart of God.

Date:

Date:

Q: J-R, I've heard that you suggest that all of your initiates chant their tones for two hours a day. That seems like a long time, and I'm really having difficulty doing that. How can I do better?

A: The two-hour suggestion for spiritual exercises is just that, a suggestion. The expectation is not that everyone will immediately be able to sustain two hours, although that would be very nice. But two hours is the goal you're moving toward. Achieving that may be gradual; that's okay. Don't get down on yourself and create patterns of guilt for not being able to do that instantly. Take your time, take it easy. Love yourself. Love the Traveler. Let it unfold in its own timing, but keep in mind that two hours is your goal and move actively toward that.

Date:

Date:

Q: When I begin to chant my tone, sometimes the energy comes in so intensely that everything goes into revolt. I feel restless and want to get up and start moving around. Is there some way I can keep this from happening?

A: The way you learn to hold spiritual energy is just to keep doing it and doing it and doing it. In the beginning, it may seem like you can't hold the energy for very long, and that's to be expected. As you continue working with the tones, you'll be able to hold a little longer and a little longer. And as you can hold the energy for a longer period, more energy will come in. Then there will be another shift as you learn to handle more. It's a continuous process—continuous growth. And being able to hold the spiritual energies is really a great, great blessing.

Date:

Date:

Q: *You suggest that after chanting, we listen quietly for a while. I find that when I listen, I begin to daydream. What would you suggest?*

A: *The listening portion of spiritual exercises can seem like a nebulous thing and the way you choose to do it can be developed through experimentation and your own intuition. If you find yourself doing nothing but daydreaming, you can work on consciously focusing your mind into the tone rather than into the fantasies. If the daydream occurs infrequently or you sense that you are still chanting the tone, you needn't be too concerned about it. You may be releasing karma or clearing past events. The idea is to focus on the tone, so when you notice you're into other things, you can just move your focus back to the tone. You might do this often during one sitting. It takes practice, so be patient with yourself. Just relax into the process.*

Date:

Date:

Q: *Is the discipline of doing spiritual exercises regularly going to raise my level of consciousness and free me of karma?*

A: *A partial yes. The other part of it involves your attitude toward your spiritual exercises. If you do them as a form of punishment, as martyrdom or complaining, spiritual exercises may not do too much. But if you do them in a form of sacredness and holiness and use them as a spiritual time between you and God, the answer to your question is yes. Absolutely.*

Date:

Date:

Q: *What is the purpose of existence after reaching the highest realm?*

A: *For the most part, the goal of every Soul on the planet is to become a co-creator with God. In one sense, God needs us as much as we need God. We are how God gets things done on this physical-material level. He works through us in this world. The human body and consciousness are receptors for Spirit on this level; they are what the Soul uses to transport itself here.*

But on the other levels, there are a lot of jobs that you might be assigned to fulfill. You could work in another dimension, another universe. If you have elevated yourself in a certain way within a certain schooling pattern, you could just live within a section of the higher realms of Light where a lot of equally-evolved Souls live. It's awfully hard to put words on this kind of action. As soon as I try, it sounds like a lie because I'm trying to put into vocabulary that which is beyond words. I'm really trying to give you the feeling of it, the essence of it, hoping you'll bypass the intellectual confusion and reach in to see the reality of it.

Date:

Q: *Does my service or any of my actions in the world affect my initiation? Is there anything I can do (besides s.e.'s) to help me get through each level to my next initiation?*

A: *No, the initiation is to the higher levels of Light. The more you chant your initiatory tone, the more you are affected on the inside of you. Some of the changes will be so subtle that you might not even notice them at first. Then you might find that you are being of service more and more or that your attitude has changed.*

All you really have to do is your spiritual exercises, live your life and keep your eyes open. The inner awareness will come to you as you participate in your life and the situations that are presented to you daily.

Date:
_____

_____

_____

_____

_____

_____

_____

_____

_____

_____

Date:

Q: *What can I do to keep from being psychically influenced when I am asleep?*

A: *When you go to bed, take a few minutes before going to sleep and ask for the Light to be with you throughout the night and that it protect you in the other dimensions. Tell yourself that if you see anything negative (whether it has to do with you personally or situations in the world or whatever) you will immediately, in your dreams, ask for the Light and protection, and use that Light to disperse any negativity. If you are an initiate, nothing can harm you because the Traveler is with you.*

Date:

Date:

Q: *I often hear people talk about nightly "soul trains" which leave at midnight. Does this mean that if I'm not asleep by midnight I miss my chance to go to the Soul realm with the Traveler that night?*

A: *There is a midnight "train" in which I collect the votaries to travel the inner realms. But if you miss that one, there is another at 2 a.m. The most important thing is not so much what time you go to sleep as it is your attitude. I suggest before you go to sleep you quickly review your day. Learn where you might have handled things in greater neutrality and loving, and forgive yourself wherever necessary. Then ask that the Traveler work with you during the sleep/dream state for the highest good.*

Date:

Date:

Q: I've been having a lot of bad dreams at night. When I wake up, I'm really frightened and sometimes shaking, and it can take hours to get myself back into balance and to sleep again. Can you suggest anything?

A: Your dreams could be all sorts of things: clearing karma, working through unconscious or subconscious fears, blocks, etc., particularly when the Mystical Traveler Consciousness is working with you. Whatever they are, don't give them a lot of power. If you wake up after a bad dream, just go to work with yourself. Chant your tone or the HU or the Ani-Hu. Surround yourself with the Light. Ask for the Mystical Traveler to help you release the dream experience. Keep some water by your bed and drink a little of it to break the intensity of the dream experience and to help you come back into the body. There is also a tone of "E" that you can chant which will help to bring you back into physical focus. You just say "eeeeeeeeeee"—a long, drawn out sound. You start the sound low, at your feet, and take it up as high as you can, over the top of your head, then drop it back down as low as you can, to the bottom of your feet. That will help to bring you back solidly into the physical level. Exercise can also break the unbalanced feeling from "bad dreams."

Date:
_____

_____

_____

_____

_____

Date:

Q: *When I'm working off karma, is there a way that I can be assured that I'm not going to create more?*

A: *Do all things in God's name. Place the Light ahead of you in all that you do. Ask always that your actions be for the highest good. You may accrue some karma, but it will be worked off that night in the sleep state and cleared instantly through the grace of the Traveler.*

This works only if your actions reflect living love, not ego involvement. The best way not to accrue karma is to remain neutral. If you make a mistake, don't feel guilty about it; if possible, go back and clear the mistake. If you have a misunderstanding with someone, just talk to them and clear it with them. Often, karma is produced more by guilt than by the actions themselves. So either enjoy it or don't do it.

Date:
_____

_____

_____

_____

_____

_____

_____

_____

_____

_____

Date:

Q: **What can you do to stop my negativity?**

A: It's not what I can do; it's what you can do. The thing that changes negative into positive is the willingness to do just that. No one is going to do it for you; you have to do it yourself. The Traveler will go through it with you and hold with you, but you must make the change, and as soon as you turn inside the Traveler is there supporting the positive. It's amazing that each time you move from the negative to the positive it gets easier and easier, and pretty soon you are spending most of your time in positive patterns.

Date:

Date:

Q: *I've heard that after we've done one negative thing—like yelling at someone—it takes twenty-five positive things to balance it. Is that true?*

A: *Yes, it's twenty-five positives to one negative to neutralize it—not to erase it, but to neutralize it. That's the law. So if you start yelling at somebody, you may need to do up to three or four hundred positive things just to neutralize the effects of that yelling.*

But instead of being under the law, you can come under grace. This would be something like, "I didn't know better, or I would have done better. They didn't know better, or they would have done better. And in that, I forgive myself and I forgive them. I love me, I love them, and now we move on." The Soul energy then comes forward and suspends it. It's not just neutralized; it's suspended through grace.

Date:
_____
_____
_____
_____
_____
_____
_____
_____
_____

Date:

Q: **What stops me from enjoying my life more?**

A: *You have habitual patterns, like a number of people, where you focus on the negative, you get involved in the negative, and you get fascinated by it. That's one of the elements that negativity has on our consciousness—fascination. It has an attraction, a glamour, and it holds our attention. It's allowed to do that, to have energy that our consciousness responds to, but we're larger than whatever the negativity is. So we have the ability to transcend it. Always, that ability is there. The more you know that ability and direct it to overcome, the less the negativity impacts on you. You may find that you're simply directing your energy into what serves you, into who you are. Be more willing to live your life according to your true self and not what's happening outside yourself.*

Date:

Date:

Q: I'm working on being more forgiving of myself for some of the dumb things I do. I hope that helps me to be easier on myself. What else can I do?

A: Do the best you can, and have loving as the keynote for your existence. Sometimes you'll fall short. So what? Get up and go again. The teachings say, "Do all things in loving." But when somebody doesn't do that, we don't say, "Now kill them." Instead we say, "Sometimes you fall, and when you do, get up one more time than you fall."

There is forgiveness and grace in all the teachings, and you have to forgive yourself first. If you say, "I fall short of my own standard," you might want to revise your standard to be one of harmony and balance instead of self-criticism. Anyway, the Soul, the part of you that's the Spirit part, doesn't care about what goes on because what happens is just experience, and the Soul sees it in all of its perfection.

The part that you need to be kind to is your ego, which comes out of the mind and the emotions. Because the ego is tied to your mind and emotions, if you go to beat it up, you will feel mentally and emotionally beaten up. Be kind to that part of you. Then when you go back inside, you will feel the kindness in your emotions and your mind.

Demonstrate the loving to yourself. When you eat well, you are demonstrating the loving for your body. When you exercise your body to utilize the energy better, you are also demonstrating the loving for your body. As you think positive thoughts, you are demonstrating the loving for your mind. As you do things to keep the emotions harmoniously balanced, you are demonstrating the loving for the emotions. When you start to do these things, you'll live in greater balance and joy, and other people will be attracted into that force of love.

Date:

Q: *I see that part of why I get sick is so I can have some time off to be in bed and read discourses and listen to seminar tapes, which is really what I like to do. How can I work with that?*

A: *You don't need an excuse to do what you want to do. All you have to say is, "I'm going to do this now. I'm nurturing the spiritual part of me." You don't have to get sick to do what you want to do.*

We all want to listen to tapes and read discourses, but we'll often put it off and not find time. When we're sick, we have a great time to do those things. So we use our sick time for up-time. Free-form writing during that sick period also helps clear out the junk. But the important thing to remember is that you don't need an excuse to do what you want to do. You can just go do it.

Date:

Date:

Q: Are there angels in the Soul realm? What exactly is an angel, and what is a guardian angel?

A: There are angels on every non-physical level. Some people have seen angels on this physical level, although they are actually seeing into another level when this happens. Angels are non-physical beings who hold spiritual energy and do spiritual work on the different levels of existence. One of their "jobs" is to praise God continuously; it's very joyful.

A guardian angel has a specific job—to assist, guide, and protect a certain person. The guardian angel is one who will urge and direct; it works like a sort of reflective counselor. When you work with it, it can be effective. People who have been baptized within MSIA and certain faiths or groups have had a guardian angel placed with them at the time of baptism.

Date:

Date:

Q: *What does it mean when I see blue or purple lights around people?*

A: *The Mystical Traveler Consciousness often comes in on a purple light. It represents transmutation, which is a function of the Traveler—to transmute the negativity of this world into the positivity of Spirit. Seeing purple often indicates that the spiritual form of the Traveler is present and a special blessing is being extended. Blue is often a color indicating Spirit or the presence of spiritual energy.*

Date:

Date:

Q: **Can you help me with the doubt I feel?**

A: *You can use your doubt as a prover, as a tool to inquire, and your inquiry needs to be critical. Not negative, critical. That means looking very closely and precisely at something instead of just running your doubt as information or evidence. Doubt has no information or evidence in it. It has a feeling that things don't fit. If you have that feeling, you then use your intelligence to go in and see either how things do fit or what does not fit. Now you've proven something for yourself. Either way, your doubt has served you.*

Date:

Date:

Q: *How can I assist others while maintaining my own balance?*

A: *Before reaching out to another, call in the Light of the Holy Spirit and ask that this Light surround, protect and fill you. Then ask that the Light surround, fill and protect the other person so that only that which is for the highest good may come forward. Ask for the guidance of the Light and of the Traveler and then listen for that guidance inwardly. As you learn to tune into your own inner guidance, you will learn to recognize that inner knower, the part of you that knows what is right for you in every situation. You have only but to tune into it, trust yourself, and check out what you hear.*

Date:

Date:

Q: *Why do I feel drained in group situations?*

A: *You haven't got your polarity in motion so that you give and receive equally. You're probably giving too much of yourself, even unconsciously. One way to balance this would be to sit with one hand facing down and the other one facing up and then switch until you find out which one is pulling energy in for you. You can do this whenever you get a chance. You can actually feel the energy coming in toward you. When you do this, keep your feet crossed so the energy does not dissipate or drain from you again. This technique can help to balance your energies and you should not feel so drained.*

Date:

Date:

Q: *I feel really low in energy and I don't know why. I've seen health practitioners, and there doesn't seem to be anything wrong physically, but I just can't seem to get the energy up to do anything.*

A: *Remember that you get what you create. If you think too much about that which is negative, you'll create that. So keep your thoughts positive and your energy flowing upward. You might also want to check out your diet (physical, mental, and emotional), not only to see what you're eating, but also to see what's eating you.*

Date:

Date:

Q: *It's very easy for me to give and give, but much more difficult for me to receive. How can I learn to receive?*

A: *You must be open to receive. If I have something to give you but your hands are tightly closed behind your back, I have no vessel in which to place my gift. But if your hands are open and you reach out to receive, I can place the gift in them.*

The same is true for those things that are of Spirit. If you are uptight and closed down inside of yourself, how can you be open to receive the bounty that is available to you?

If it's truly difficult to receive, you might begin by receiving in small ways. Let someone buy you lunch, open the door or run an errand for you. Most people will be very willing to give to you. It's you who decides how much you want to receive on all levels.

Date:

Date:

Q: *When Jesus said, "It is easier for a camel to pass through the eye of a needle," did he mean that material wealth automatically pulls you away from the spiritual?*

A: *Being* attached *to the accumulation of material wealth might be a deterrent to discovering the more spiritual aspects of yourself. But material wealth can also be an outer reflection of the inner wealth and abundance that you are experiencing inside of yourself. There is nothing "wrong" with having material possessions. Sometimes they can assist you to live a more comfortable life so that you can more easily be of service to others. And many times* sharing *the abundance of your material possessions can be beneficial to others. It's all in how you handle it inside of yourself.*

Date:

Date:

Q: *How does diet affect spirituality?*

A: *Let me answer this way: it matters very little what you eat or how much you eat or if you fast or if you drink only liquids or any other diet variation. These are physical patterns that do not determine whether or not you will see the face of God. If one type of diet makes you feel more comfortable than another while you are on your way to God, then it is working for you and it's the one to follow. If you find out that it ceases to work for you, if it begins to look like a detour or a maze with a dead end, then it is no longer working for you and it is probably time to change. Only you can know for sure what is and is not working for you. Let that be your guide.*

Date:

Date:

Q: *How can I know if the inner answers I hear are from you or from my imagination?*

A: *I have always taught all votaries to check everything out. If the information works for you and does not inflict on anyone else, use it. Who cares whether it was from me or from your imagination? If you lean into the information received and it doesn't work for you, then don't follow it. And again, who cares where it came from? If it doesn't work, it doesn't work. Another "checkpoint" is the idea of, If in doubt, don't do. Hold, don't take action, ask inwardly for greater clarification, and then see what happens next.*

You can also check the accuracy of your inner answers by referring to the outer teachings. The inner guidance will always complement the outer teachings, and the Traveler will not counsel any action that would harm or hurt you or anyone else. So if you hear inner guidance toward an action that will be inflictive or harmful to you or any other human being, just know that is not the Traveler.

Contact with the Traveler inwardly will often bring with it a warmth and a feeling of loving protection.

Date:

Date:

Q: *I seem to be fairly smart intellectually, but I'm often off when it comes to "gut level" knowing. How can I increase my gut level intuitive knowing?*

A: *That type of knowledge comes with time and patience. Experiment with your intuition, then check its accuracy. It may involve a process of watching or trial and error.*

You may want to test your ability with those whom you know will support and love you and with whom you feel safe. As you feel better about yourself and are less concerned about what other people think about you, you become more aware of your own sense of Self. You can then tune into the "Self" anytime you want. The true Self is the knower you are looking for. Just relax and gain confidence in yourself.

Date:

Date:

Q: *What do you mean when you say, "God is intention"?*

A: *God has purpose. Spirit has purpose. When you have purpose, you have an intention. And where intention comes from is intent. Think about that and you realize that God is always giving. Mankind is always taking. That's where you have uncertainty in your spiritual life. You keep taking and taking, and you know that you can't take enough to fill the place where Spirit resides.*

We're taught physically, emotionally, and mentally to be takers, and yet what's giving life to us? Our Spirit. Our giver. It doesn't care if you love it, if you hate it, if you disagree, if you're upset—whatever. It just keeps giving. As you attune to the Spirit in you, you do take at first. Then you start giving. You find that the giving brings you into more of the experience of Spirit within you.

Date:

Date:

Q: *I'm afraid of dying. Can you help me with this?*

A: *You haven't contacted the Spirit inside of you. As soon as you do, that fear of dying will be a process of breathing. Look at it this way. Life is like a game; we're tossed out into it with a very short period of time to learn anything, and a whole lot of lack of ability and equipment. And death is the winner—we are all going to die. From the moment you take your first breath, death is on your tail. I call this the hounds of hell. But there are hounds of heaven, too, called the Travelers, and they're also stalking you.*

Those who are stalking the Spirit are attempting to bypass the rules of death's game and slip past the bonds of death into the Light, and live in that particular perspective. Therefore, loving, sharing, and caring are not what death deals with. Death does not deal with health, wealth, and happiness, nor does it deal with prosperity, abundance, and riches. It deals with obliterating your consciousness from this level. So while you're doing these other things, death does not recognize you. If you can leave your body and transcend to the Spirit, death mistakes you as being part of its spiritual beingness and leaves you alone. So when you die, you don't die the second death, you just die the death of the body.

If you slip, you'll hear the hounds of hell bark, and the "what-if's" of your mind start running, "Oh my God, maybe I'll die. Maybe I'll fall." Then death goes, "There you are. I see you," and starts to hone in on you. You have to clear that, and you can do it through prayer, meditation, contemplation, spiritual exercises, being of service, loving people, et cetera.

I'd stalk the Spirit of life. And the one we call the Christ. How does the Christ appear? Any way It wants to. It could come as the cleansing of the temple or the one who is wiping away your tears. How will you know how It's going to come to you? By the way you are when It comes. Remember that the Traveler and the Christ are at their best when you are at your worst. When you're at your best, you're also being in the Christ.

Date:

Q: *I've heard you use the words "Baruch Bashan" at the end of your seminars. What do these words mean?*

A: *They are Hebrew and they mean "the blessings already are." That means exactly what it says and if you look at the meaning of those words, you will realize the power of that statement. The blessings are already around you and all you have to do is open yourself up to the possibility of receiving them.*

Date:

Date:

Q: *I know I pay too much attention to what other people think about what I do or say. Can you help me with this?*

A: *Why be concerned about what somebody else is saying or thinking or following or doing? The most important thing that I could emphasize is that it does not matter what I or anyone else says. The only thing that matters is what you say to yourself in your Spirit as you lift and encourage yourself.*

Do you know what the key phrase is in the Bible? Praise God. Do you know what you do when you praise God? You lift yourself up. Calling God into you through your eyes and your voice brings the convergence of the Spirit, when you are filled with the Holy Spirit. Your whole life takes on a different aspect, and you must be prepared for the world to start rejecting and ridiculing you. This can be your family, your friends, the people you work with. But one day they are going to come to that place themselves, and they will say, Thank you for holding to what you knew. Thank you for standing strong when the winds and the tempest blew. Thank you for disregarding what others said and following what you knew in your heart to be true because there lies the way for all of us to overcome the uncertainties and struggles of life. There lies the path of finding the certainty of our own beingness, and living in that. That's what I would wish for all of you.

Baruch Bashan

Date:

Date:

Date:

Date:

Baruch Bashan